KU-021-603

WHERE'S WALLY?
THE
FANTASTIC JOURNEY

MARTIN HANDFORD

THE GOBBLING GLUTTONS

ONCE UPON A TIME WALLY
EMBARKED UPON A FANTASTIC
JOURNEY. FIRST, AMONG A
THRONG OF GOBBLING GLUTTONS,
HE MET WIZARD WHITEBEARD, WHO
COMMANDED HIM TO FIND A SCROLL AND
THEN TO FIND ANOTHER AT EVERY STAGE OF
HIS JOURNEY, FOR WHEN HE HAD FOUND
12 SCROLLS, HE WOULD UNDERSTAND THE
TRUTH ABOUT HIMSELF.

IN EVERY PICTURE FIND WALLY, WOOF (BUT ALL
YOU CAN SEE IS HIS TAIL), WENDA, WIZARD
WHITEBEARD, ODLAW AND THE SCROLL. THEN
FIND WALLY'S KEY, WOOF'S BONE (IN THIS SCENE
IT'S THE BONE THAT'S NEAREST TO HIS TAIL),
WENDA'S CAMERA AND ODLAW'S BINOCULARS.

THERE ARE ALSO 25 WALLY-WATCHERS, EACH OF
WHOM APPEARS ONLY ONCE SOMEWHERE IN
THE FOLLOWING 12 PICTURES. AND ONE MORE
THING! CAN YOU FIND ANOTHER CHARACTER,
NOT SHOWN BELOW, WHO APPEARS ONCE IN
EVERY PICTURE EXCEPT THE LAST?

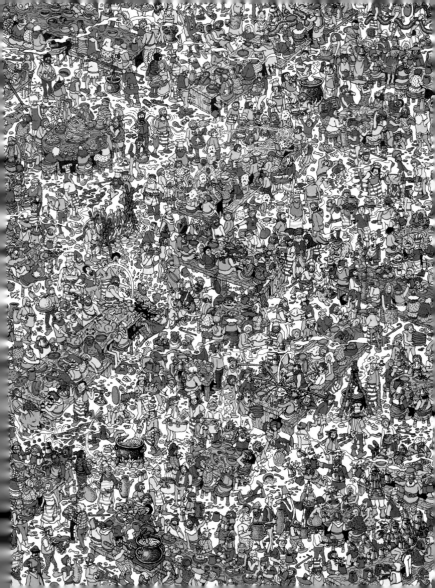

THE BATTLING MONKS

THEN WALLY AND WIZARD WHITEBEARD CAME
TO THE PLACE WHERE THE INVISIBLE MONKS
OF FIRE FOUGHT THE MONKS OF WATER. AND
AS WALLY SEARCHED FOR THE SECOND SCROLL,
HE SAW THAT MANY WALLIES HAD BEEN THIS WAY BEFORE.
AND WHEN HE FOUND THE SCROLL, IT WAS TIME TO
CONTINUE WITH HIS JOURNEY.

THE DRAGON FLYERS

THEN WALLY AND WIZARD WHITEBEARD CAME
TO THE LAND OF THE DRAGON FLYERS, WHERE
MANY WALLIES HAD BEEN BEFORE. AND WALLY
SAW A COLOURFUL FLEET OF DRAGONS AND
FLYERS WEARING DRAGON-TAIL HOODS FILLING THE SKY.
THERE ARE ARROW SHAPES APLENTY TO SPOT IN THIS TALE OF
TAILS. OH BRAINY DRAGON WATCHERS. AND WHEN WALLY FOUND
THE THIRD SCROLL, IT WAS TIME TO CONTINUE HIS JOURNEY.

THE GREAT BALL-GAME PLAYERS

THEN WALLY AND WIZARD WHITEBEARD CAME TO
THE PLAYING FIELD OF THE GREAT BALL-GAME
PLAYERS, WHERE MANY WALLIES HAD BEEN BEFORE.
AND WALLY SAW THAT FOUR TEAMS WERE PLAYING AGAINST
EACH OTHER (BUT WAS ANYONE WINNING? WHAT WAS THE
SCORE? CAN YOU WORK OUT THE RULES?). THEN WALLY FOUND
THE FOURTH SCROLL AND CONTINUED WITH HIS JOURNEY.

THE FEROCIOUS RED DWARVES

THEN WALLY AND WIZARD WHITEBEARD
CAME AMONG THE FEROCIOUS RED DWARVES,
WHERE MANY WALLIES HAD BEEN BEFORE.
AND THE DWARVES WERE ATTACKING THE MANY-
COLOURED SPEARMEN, CAUSING MIGHTY MAYHEM AND
HORRID HAVOC. AND WALLY FOUND THE FIFTH SCROLL
AND CONTINUED WITH HIS JOURNEY.

THE NASTY NASTIES

THEN WALLY AND WIZARD WHITEBEARD
CAME TO THE CASTLE OF THE NASTY NASTIES,
WHERE MANY WALLIES HAD BEEN BEFORE. AND
WHEREVER WALLY WALKED, THERE WAS A CLATTERING
OF BONES (WOOF'S BONE IN THIS SCENE IS THE NEAREST TO
HIS TAIL) AND A FOUL SLURPING OF FILTHY FOOD. AND WALLY
FOUND THE SIXTH SCROLL AND CONTINUED WITH HIS JOURNEY.

THE FIGHTING FORESTERS

THEN WALLY AND WIZARD WHITEBEARD CAME
AMONG THE FIGHTING FORESTERS, WHERE
MANY WALLIES HAD BEEN BEFORE. AND IN
THEIR BATTLE WITH THE EVIL BLACK KNIGHTS, THE
FOREST WOMEN WERE AIDED BY THE ANIMALS, BY THE LIVING
MUD, EVEN BY THE TREES THEMSELVES. AND WALLY FOUND THE
SEVENTH SCROLL AND CONTINUED WITH HIS JOURNEY.

THE DEEP-SEA DIVERS

THEN WALLY AND WIZARD WHITEBEARD CAME TO THE WATERY WORLD OF THE DEEP-SEA DIVERS, WHERE MANY WALLIES HAD BEEN BEFORE. AND WALLY SEARCHED FOR THE EIGHTH SCROLL AMONG THE MONSTERS OF THE DEEP, AMONG THE MERMAIDS, FISHERMEN AND FISH. AND WHEN HE FOUND IT, IT WAS TIME TO CONTINUE WITH HIS JOURNEY.

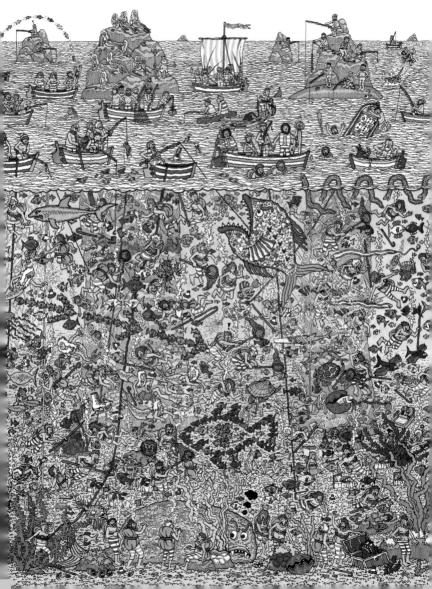

THE KNIGHTS OF THE MAGIC FLAG

THEN WALLY AND WIZARD WHITEBEARD CAME TO A PLACE MORE CROWDED THAN ANY WALLY HAD SEEN BEFORE, WHERE TWO ARMIES WITH MANY MAGIC FLAGS WERE LOCKED IN COMBAT. AND WALLY SAW THAT MANY WALLIES HAD BEEN THIS WAY BEFORE. AND WHEN HE FOUND THE NINTH SCROLL, IT WAS TIME TO CONTINUE WITH HIS JOURNEY.

THE UNFRIENDLY GIANTS

THEN WALLY AND WIZARD WHITEBEARD CAME TO THE LAND OF THE UNFRIENDLY GIANTS, WHERE MANY WALLIES HAD BEEN BEFORE, AND WALLY SAW THAT THE GIANTS WERE HORRIDLY HARASSING THE LITTLE PEOPLE. AND WHEN HE FOUND THE TENTH SCROLL, IT WAS TIME TO CONTINUE WITH HIS JOURNEY.

THE UNDERGROUND HUNTERS

THEN WALLY AND WIZARD WHITEBEARD CAME AMONG THE UNDERGROUND HUNTERS, WHERE MANY WALLIES HAD BEEN BEFORE. AND THERE WAS MUCH MENACE IN THIS PLACE, AND A MULTITUDE OF MALEVOLENT MONSTERS. AND WALLY FOUND THE ELEVENTH SCROLL AND CONTINUED WITH HIS JOURNEY.

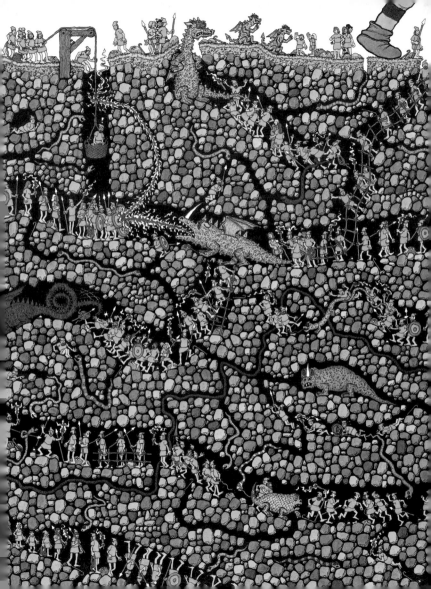

THE LAND OF WALLIES

THEN WALLY FOUND THE TWELFTH SCROLL AND SAW THE
TRUTH ABOUT HIMSELF, THAT HE WAS JUST ONE WALLY
AMONG MANY. HE SAW TOO THAT WALLIES OFTEN LOSE
THINGS, FOR HE HIMSELF HAD LOST ONE SHOE. AND AS
HE LOOKED FOR HIS SHOE, HE DISCOVERED THAT WIZARD
WHITEBEARD WAS NOT HIS ONLY FELLOW TRAVELLER. THERE WERE
NOW ELEVEN OTHERS - ONE FROM EVERY PLACE HE HAD BEEN TO -
WHO HAD JOINED HIM ONE BY ONE ALONG THE WAY. SO NOW (OH LOYAL
FOLLOWERS OF WALLY!) FIND THE REAL WALLY AND HELP HIM FIND HIS
MISSING SHOE. AND THERE, IN THE LAND OF WALLIES,
MAY WALLY LIVE HAPPILY EVER AFTER.

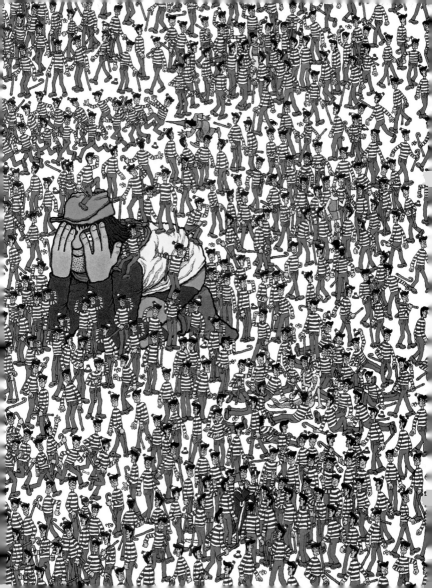

THE WHERE'S WALLY? FANTASTIC JOURNEY CHECKLIST
Hundreds more things for Wally followers to look for!

THE GOBBLING GLUTTONS
- A strong waiter and a weak one
- Long-distance smells
- Unequal portions of pie
- A man who has had too much to drink
- People who are going the wrong way
- Very tough dishes
- An upside-down dish
- Knights drinking through straws
- A very hot dinner
- A clever drink-pourer
- Giant sausages
- A custard fight
- An overloaded seat
- Beard-flavoured soup
- Men pulling legs
- A painful spillage
- A man tied up in spaghetti
- A knock-out dish
- A man who has eaten too much
- A tall diner eating a tall dish
- An exploding pie
- A giant sausage breaking in half
- A smell travelling through two people
- A bear shield

THE BATTLING MONKS
- Two fire engines
- Hot-footed monks
- A bridge made of monks
- A cheeky monk
- A diving monk
- A scared statue
- Fire meeting water
- A snaking jet of water
- Chasers being chased
- A smug statue
- A snaking jet of flame
- A five-way wash-out
- A burning bridge
- Seven burning backsides
- Monks worshipping the Flowing Bucket of Water
- Monks shielding themselves from lava
- Thirteen trapped and extremely worried monks
- A monk seeing an oncoming jet of flame
- Monks worshipping the Mighty Erupting Volcano
- A very worried monk confronted by two opponents
- A burning hose
- Monks and lava pouring out of a volcano
- A chain of water
- Two monks accidentally attacking their brothers

THE DRAGON FLYERS
- Two dragons on a collision course
- A pedestrian crossing
- Two hangers-on
- Four hitchhikers
- Salesmen selling young dragons
- Dragon flyer highwaymen
- A concussed dragon
- Dragon cops and robbers
- Upside-down flyers
- A dragon beauty parlour
- A flying tower
- A dragon-tail staircase
- A topsy-turvy tower
- Dragons in love
- Flyers with dragon-tail-shaped beards
- Five extra-long red bus dragons
- A tail fight
- A passenger with empty pockets
- Queues at three bus dragon stops
- One person wearing two red shoes
- A dragon flying backwards
- A dragon indoors
- Two suddenly dragonless riders

THE GREAT BALL-GAME PLAYERS
- A three-way drink
- A chase that goes round in circles
- A backside shot
- A spectator surrounded by three rival supporters
- A row of hand-held banners
- Two tall players versus short ones
- A shot that breaks the woodwork
- A mob chasing a player backwards
- Players who are digging for victory
- A face about to hit a fist
- Seven awful singers
- A face made of balls
- A player chasing a mob
- Players pulling each other's hoods
- A flag with a hole in it
- A mob of players all holding balls
- A player heading a ball
- A player tripping over a rock
- A player punching a ball
- A spectator accidentally hitting two others
- A player poking his tongue out at a mob
- A mouth pulled open by a beard
- Players who can't see where they are going

THE FEROCIOUS RED DWARVES
- A spear-breaking slingshot
- Two punches causing chain reactions
- Fat and thin spears and spearmen
- A spearman being knocked through a flag
- A collar made out of a shield
- A prison made of spears
- A spearman trapped by his battle dress
- An axe-head causing headaches
- Dwarves disguised as spearmen
- Opponents charging through each other
- A spearman running away from a spear
- A sneaky spear-bender
- A devious disarmer
- A dwarf who is on the wrong side
- Cheeky target practice
- A stick-up machine
- Tangled spears
- A slingshot causing a chain reaction
- A sword cutting through a shield
- A spear hitting a spearman's shield
- A dwarf hiding up a spear
- A spear knocking off a dwarf's helmet
- Spearmen who have jumped out of their clothes

THE NASTY NASTIES
- A vampire who is scared of ghosts
- A dancing mummy
- Vampires drinking through straws
- Gargoyle lovers
- An upside-down torture
- A baseball bat
- Three wolfmen
- A mummy who is coming undone
- Dog, cat and mouse doorways
- A vampire mirror test
- A frightened skeleton
- A ghoulish game of skittles
- A gargoyle being poked on the nose
- An upside-down gargoyle
- Fang-tastic flight controllers
- Three witches flying backwards
- A witch losing her broomstick
- A broomstick flying a witch
- A ticklish torture
- A vampire about to get the chop
- A ghost train
- A vampire who doesn't fit his coffin
- A three-eyed, hooded torturer

THE FIGHTING FORESTERS

- [ ] Three long legs
- [ ] Knights shooting arrows at knights
- [ ] Knights being chopped down by a tree
- [ ] Two multiple knock-outs
- [ ] Eight pairs of upside-down feet
- [ ] A tree with a lot of puff
- [ ] Hard-headed women
- [ ] Attackers about to be attacked
- [ ] A strong woman and a weak one
- [ ] An easily frightened horse
- [ ] A lazy lady
- [ ] A three-legged knight
- [ ] An upside-down ladder
- [ ] Loving trees
- [ ] An upside-down trunk
- [ ] A two-headed unicorn
- [ ] A unicorn in a tree
- [ ] Foliage faces
- [ ] Muddy mud-slingers
- [ ] A tearful small tree
- [ ] Spears getting sharpened tips
- [ ] Trees branching out violently
- [ ] Stilts being chewed up

THE DEEP-SEA DIVERS

- [ ] A two-headed fish
- [ ] A sword fight with a swordfish
- [ ] Fish fingers
- [ ] A sea bed
- [ ] A fish face
- [ ] A catfish and a dogfish
- [ ] A jellyfish
- [ ] A fish with two tails
- [ ] Two fish-shaped formations
- [ ] A sea-lion
- [ ] A skate
- [ ] Treacherous treasure
- [ ] Oyster-beds
- [ ] Tinned fish
- [ ] Flying fish
- [ ] Electric eels
- [ ] A deck of cards
- [ ] A bottle in a message
- [ ] A fake fin
- [ ] A back to front mermaid
- [ ] A seahorse-drawn carriage
- [ ] A boat's compass
- [ ] A fish fishing
- [ ] An underwater beach scene
- [ ] Divers drawing on an angry sea monster

THE KNIGHTS OF THE MAGIC FLAG

- [ ] Unfaithful royals
- [ ] A flag full of fists
- [ ] A game of noughts and crosses
- [ ] A sword-fighting reindeer
- [ ] A man among lions
- [ ] A mouse behind bars
- [ ] Flags within a flag
- [ ] A tangle of tongues
- [ ] A flag covered in axes
- [ ] A zebra crossing
- [ ] A puffing spoilsport
- [ ] A battering-ram door key
- [ ] Snakes and ladders
- [ ] A flame-throwing dragon
- [ ] Diminishing puddings
- [ ] A crown thief
- [ ] A thirsty lion
- [ ] A weapons imbalance
- [ ] A foot being tickled by a leather
- [ ] Some cheeky soldiers
- [ ] A surrendering reindeer
- [ ] A dog straining to get a bone
- [ ] A helmet with three eyes

THE LAND OF WALLIES

- [ ] Wallies waving
- [ ] Wallies walking
- [ ] Wallies running
- [ ] Wallies sitting
- [ ] Wallies lying down
- [ ] Wallies standing still
- [ ] Wallies giving the thumbs-up
- [ ] Wallies looking frightened
- [ ] Wallies searching
- [ ] Wallies being chased
- [ ] Wallies smiling
- [ ] Wallies sliding
- [ ] Wallies with bobble hats
- [ ] Wallies without bobble hats
- [ ] Wallies raising their bobble hats
- [ ] Wallies with walking sticks
- [ ] Wallies without walking sticks
- [ ] Wallies with spectacles
- [ ] Wallies without spectacles
- [ ] A Wally on a hat
- [ ] A Wally holding a wing
- [ ] Wally

THE UNDERGROUND HUNTERS

- [ ] A hunter about to put his foot in it
- [ ] Four frightened flames
- [ ] A snaky hat thief
- [ ] An underground traffic policeman
- [ ] Three surrendering flames
- [ ] A two-headed snake
- [ ] A ridiculously long snake
- [ ] A dragon that attacks with both ends
- [ ] Three dragons wearing sunglasses
- [ ] A snaky tickle
- [ ] Angry snake-parents
- [ ] Five broken spears
- [ ] A monstrous bridge
- [ ] Five rock faces
- [ ] Upside-down hunters
- [ ] A snake that is trapped
- [ ] A very long ladder
- [ ] A torch setting fire to spears
- [ ] Hunters tripped by a tongue
- [ ] A hunter with an extra-long spear
- [ ] Hunters about to collide
- [ ] Hunters going round in a circle
- [ ] A shocked tail-puller

THE UNFRIENDLY GIANTS

- [ ] Trappers about to be trapped
- [ ] A catapulted missile hitting people
- [ ] Three people in a giant hood
- [ ] Ducks out of water
- [ ] A mocking giant about to be struck
- [ ] A giant with a roof over his head
- [ ] Two giants who are out for the count
- [ ] Two windmill knock-outs
- [ ] A polite giant about to get a headache
- [ ] Two broom trees
- [ ] A hairy bird's nest
- [ ] A battering-ram fist
- [ ] A house-shaker
- [ ] People taking part in a board game
- [ ] A landslide of boulders
- [ ] A drawing-pin trap
- [ ] Six people loading two slingshots
- [ ] Six people strapped inside giant belts
- [ ] Rope-pullers being pulled
- [ ] Birds being disturbed by a giant
- [ ] Two game-watchers slapping people
- [ ] Four shy ladies being flattered
- [ ] A powerful burst of pond water

THE FANTASTIC JOURNEY

Did you find Wally, his friends and all the things which they had lost? Did you find the mystery character who appeared in every scene except the land of Wallies? It may be difficult, but keep searching and eventually you'll find him – now that's a clue! And one last thing: somewhere one of the Wally-watchers lost the bobble from their hat. Can you spot which one, and find the bobble!

ONE LAST THING ...

Now turn the page to play four magical puzzles! Wow!

WHICH WITCH IS WHICH?

Read the witchy riddles and match them to the pictures.

MYSTIC MARTHA PLAYS A BRILLIANT BROOM TUNE.

NOISY NORMA LIKES TO WAKE THE DEAD.

WICKED WARTIE WEARS A CLOAK AT NIGHT, AND ITS COLOUR RHYMES WITH FRIGHT.

TANGLE TOES TINA TRIPS EVERYWHERE SHE GOES.

MOORB HCTIW RIDES HER BROOM IN A PECULIAR WAY.

SOMETHING FISHY

Match up the sets of three identically coloured fish. One fish is not part of a set, so have a splish-splashing time finding out which one!

SPELL-TACULAR!

These four words have stretched out in a spectacular star shape.
Can you train your eyes to read them?

START HERE!

Clue: hold the book in front of your nose and tilt it backwards. Read the word in front of you, then turn the book to the right and read the next word and so on.

GIANT GAME

Start on the board game square next to each player's picture.
Then follow their footstep guide to work out who picks up the scroll.

BOOK IN
FOR YOUR NEW ADVENTURE TODAY

CELEBRATING WORLD BOOK DAY
20
2 MARCH 2017

3 brilliant ways to continue YOUR reading adventure

1 VISIT YOUR LOCAL BOOKSHOP

Your go-to destination for awesome reading recommendations and events with your favourite authors and illustrators.

FIND YOUR LOCAL BOOKSHOP **Booksellers.org.uk/ bookshopsearch**

2 JOIN YOUR LOCAL LIBRARY

Browse and borrow from a huge selection of books, get expert ideas of what to read next, and take part in wonderful family reading activities – all for FREE!

FIND YOUR LOCAL LIBRARY **Findalibrary.co.uk**

3 GO ONLINE AT WORLDBOOKDAY.COM

Fun activities, games, videos, downloads, competitions, new books galore and all the latest book news.

SPONSORED BY

NATIONAL BOOK tokens